"There Is A  o Pick"

By Ken Gibson

Copyright © 2022 Kenneth Gibson

ISBN 978-1-915787-14-9

Printed in Great Britain by
Biddles Books Limited, King's Lynn, Norfolk

Preface

While on holiday in Thailand in the 1990's I got into conversation with a taxi driver about unemployment in the country. He told me that officially there was no unemployment in Thailand because a job can always be found for people to do for anyone who wants it.

I had this demonstrated to me during the next few days while staying in a hotel in Krabi in the south of the country, where, even though the hotel was relatively quiet there seemed to be a multitude of staff. On talking to them I discovered that most were related to each other, and if a family member could not find employment, then the person with a job shared theirs with them and split the money. Therefore, everyone who wanted to work was able to and the money was shared between all the workers. Hence the phrase:

"There is always rice to pick".

Now in my seventies and retired I have been thinking about my life and work and the fact that during all that time I have never been unemployed. Because of circumstances I have had many and varied sorts of employment, but because I have always had a positive "I can do that" attitude I have always found rice to pick.

I hope you enjoy hearing about my experiences.

Chapter 1:

Child Labour

Not as dramatic as it sounds, and I can assure you I enjoyed every minute of it.

I was born in a small village on the North Norfolk coast called Stiffkey on 6th March 1945, the youngest of four children. From the age of five I attended the small village school which had just two classrooms, one for infants and one for juniors. I was lucky enough to be quite a bright student, but I can never really remember enjoying my time at school, all that bother having to learn the three R's, take part in enforced gym classes and the dreaded poetry reading.

Here I was made to feel very inferior by my teacher because of my Norfolk accent. I can remember being made to stand up in class and recite the poem "Cargoes" over and over again until I got the diction right. Let me give you an example: I was reading "Dirty British coaster with a salt caked smoke stack". While what I actually read out loud was "Dir'y Bti'ish coasta with a sal' cake' smoke stack", missing out all the T's and D's, as in "pass the bu''er" and "my hands are dir'y". I could not wait until I would be old enough to leave school and get a job.

My religious instruction was provided by Sunday School. Although my mother was Church of England and went to church every Sunday night our religious instruction depended on where we were living at the time. I was born in a small end of terrace cottage at the west end of the village, then at the age of seven we moved to a new council house at the other end. About three years later, after my grandmother died, we moved into her house back at the other end of the village again. This meant our mother sent us to whichever religious establishment was nearest. First chapel, then church, then chapel again. Once past eleven years old we were made to go the church with her.

I took my eleven plus exam, and, as was the system at the time, being a small village school, we were restricted by the number of passes we were allowed. Our school was allocated one pass. Although there were about four of us aged eleven only two were deemed to be clever enough to take the exam, so I took it with another girl. My father was told several years later that the reason I failed and the girl passed and went on to Grammar School was because her father worked in an office and he was only a labourer. I have never been able to prove this but would not be at all surprised.

My first day at secondary school in Wells-next-the-Sea continued my educational torment. I was wandering around the playing field at lunch time a bit lost and minding my own business when two girls came up to me and told me I had to go with them to the Home Economics teacher whose classroom overlooked the playground. I followed them, wondering what on earth she wanted to see me for, and on entering the classroom the teacher told me to hold out my hand. I did so and she then turned it over so the knuckles were at the top and then gave me a sharp smack across the knuckles with a ruler. She then told me to go away and "Don't do it again". I never did find out what I was supposed to have done, obviously a case of mistaken identity!

I must have been reasonably clever because I was placed in the "A" form and remained there all my school life. Even then I hated most subjects, especially maths and history. I quite enjoyed geography but my favourite subjects were English language and art. I usually had paintings and drawings that I had done exhibited on the classroom walls and have still got books of essays and short stories today that I wrote while at school.

I hated maths, mainly because the teacher was a complete tyrant, a bull of a man who shouted and screamed at his classes and would throw chalk, blackboard rubbers and even full boxes of chalk at pupils he was angry with. One day I was sitting right in front of the blackboard and he thought I was not concentrating so he tipped the complete blackboard over so it would land on my head. Luckily I was concentrating enough to put my hand up just in time to stop it hitting me. The thing we dreaded most on entering the classroom was the barked instruction. "Open your books and write one to thirty". This meant quick fired mental arithmetic. My brain would freeze.

Our Geography teacher was a very straight laced middle aged woman and she was teaching us when Sir Vivian Fuchs reached the south pole. She could not bring herself to pronounce his name in front of the class as she thought it would sound to us children like a very rude word, so she proceeded to pronounce it as a long drawn out "Fuussshhhh" which amused us even more.

Another subject we all hated was Religious Instruction, and I remember at my end of third year exams I came top of the class with a score of only nineteen percent. Thinking back I realise that we must have made that poor young lady teacher's life hell.

To add to my torment, when I started my last year at Secondary school I was made Head Boy. This separated me from my friends who were convinced I was getting preferential treatment. If we got into any trouble we would be lined up outside the headmaster's office and each one would go in and get the cane. I, however would be given a good lecture and be told I should be ashamed of myself because of my position of trust. Sometimes I longed to be given the cane like the other boys. Even though my ambition was to get out of school as soon as possible I ended my Secondary career exams with the highest score in the whole school and entry to the West Norfolk Technical College in King's Lynn.

I must not end my childhood days leaving you with the idea my life was a complete misery, far from it. Life outside school was endless pleasure. Stiffkey is right on the North Norfolk coast with miles of salt marshes and beautiful beaches, and my childhood memories, as for most people, are of endless summers and cold snowy winters. Hours spent roaming the marshes, swimming in the tidal creeks, sliding in the glorious mud and building rafts. Our parents never worried where we were as long as we were home by meal time.

One day we were caught over the marshes in a violent thunder storm, and when I arrived home my mother asked me if I was alright and what had I done during the storm. I just said we all took our clothes off and hid them under a bridge to keep them dry and then got in the water until the storm was over. Care had to be taken, however when on the marshes as it was quite easy to misread the tide as it rushed through the creeks and regularly flooded the whole marsh.

One cold winter's day I went with a friend and his adult brother over the marshes and on to the beach. We crossed over two empty creaks and continued walking. I kept telling the older brother that the tide was coming in but he said it was alright. I knew he was very short sighted but, being young, I never realised how bad it was. The strong northeast wind had brought the tide in early and when we got back to the first creek it was already in full flow and too deep to wade across. All we could do was dig a hole in the side of a sand dune and crouch down for cover from the wind. Slowly it got dark but it was still too deep to get across.

Eventually we heard shouting and, looking up, we could see lights bobbing up and down over the marsh. Half the village were out looking for us. We started to shout back and suddenly a man appeared wearing chest high waders and he proceeded to carry us boys across the creek on his shoulders. He told the adult brother he would have to wait until the tide went out.

There was a Royal Artillery Training Camp based at Stiffkey looking out over the salt marshes, and later as a child I turned my experiences into a way of earning pocket money. The soldiers used to go over the marsh for an enjoyable day out and would regularly get cut off by the tides. I was usually available to guide them off and always got a good tip.

The worst experience we had with the tides was in March 1953 when I was eight years old. Hundreds of lives were lost all along the east coast of England. Strong gales blew continually from the north and pushed in a very high tide. The wind continued to blow, holding the tide in. This meant that in the evening the second tide came in on top of the first one, pushing the water inland and flooding over one hundred miles of the coast from Lincolnshire, down through Norfolk and Suffolk to Essex. Many people were drowned in the floods and properties were completely destroyed by the waves.

It happened on a Saturday night and my mother and older sister were going to a ballet concert in the next village where my sister was performing. As the coach went down to the bridge over the river Stiffkey the driver realised there was water on the road. He stopped and started to reverse back up the road just in time before a wall of water swept in front of them and rushed up the valley and into the village.

The river emptied out onto the marshes through two sluice gates which closed when the tide was in to stop salt water getting inland. The sea was so high that the sluice bank had been completely inundated and the water was flowing over the top. My mother, sister and other villagers eventually managed to get home by tramping over the fields in the pitch dark and gales.

The next morning my father walked me and my brothers round to the sluice bank and we were met by a scene of destruction I will never forget. The sluice gates had been chained up into an open position, and to the right of us where there would normally be fields and meadows, there was water for as far as the eye could see. In the centre was an enormous whirlpool with trees and dead farm animals floating round in it. To the left of us two enormous jets of water were shooting out of the sluices, including dead animals etc., and sending them out across the marshes as the water was trying to get back out to sea again.

In the winter we went "Up the hills" to go sledging in the snow, loads of kids and parents of all ages having the time of their lives. The summer version was not so successful for me. We all had buggies made out of orange boxes and pram wheels and steered by a piece of string. One time when I was about nine, I went down a hill too fast, lost control and crashed the buggy, leaving myself laying on the ground with a broken arm while the front wheels carried on to the bottom of the hill.

The Royal Artillery training camp at Stiffkey was continually full of soldiers learning how to fire heavy guns. A plane would fly backwards and forwards over the marshes towing a red target and the soldiers would fire the guns at the target. Later they flew remote controlled drones. The soldiers were instructed to aim behind the drone and not hit them as they were very expensive. You could see how well they were doing by the puffs of smoke as the shells exploded. Sometimes they were accidentally shot down but usually they ran out of fuel and drifted serenely down onto the marshes by a silk parachute. A group of soldiers would then be dispatched over the marshes to retrieve them. Unfortunately for them we knew the marshes much better than they did and by the time they arrived the planes would be missing their parachutes, parachute cord and all useable parts. Every woman in the village had silk underwear, every man had copious supplies of unbreakable string and all the children had working Meccano sets driven by little motors that originally worked the ailerons in the wings of the drones. Later when the Americans arrived the silk and cord was replaced by nylon and the product that filled the wings which was like a very dense polystyrene was perfect for model making.

My father worked as a maintenance man on the army camp as did several of the village men until it closed in the early 1960's. It also had a superb dance hall and cinema, more of which I will come to later.

Once a cargo ship lost its load of timber in a storm and it was said that you could walk the whole length of the Stiffkey shoreline on the timber without ever getting off onto the sand. The next day the whole village were there salvaging the timber. My father, my two older brothers and I collected a huge pile of timber, roped it together and waited for the tide to come in. We then poled it down the creek on the tide to the bottom of the marsh and then carried it home. My father kept pigs and had an acre of land where he grew turnips for feed. He dug a large hole in the turnip field, buried the wood and set the turnips back on top. Being an ex-merchant seaman he knew what was going to happen. A few days later the customs men arrived and went to every house in the village and carted all the wood away that they could find. They never found my father's and a year later he was the proud owner of some very smart new pig-sties.

My first job was when I was about eleven years old, and, being a churchgoer at the insistence of my mother was the position of pumping the church organ. If I remember correctly I was paid two shillings a week. This involved sitting on a chair beside the organ, and when required the organist would say "Pump" and I would start pumping a handle up and down to fill the bellows with air. I would have to continue pumping until the hymn was ended. To say this was a monotonous job would be an understatement and more than once I would nod off and the organ would splutter into silence and the organist would shout at me "More wind!".

When I was about twelve I got a job as a Saturday delivery boy with the local butcher for ten shillings a week. I would cycle round the village on a trade bike and deliver meat to customer's houses. I loved that job and did it until I went to college at fifteen. People used to tell my parents they knew when I was coming because they could hear me whistling as I came up the road (why don't people whistle anymore?). I used to work there during my summer holidays as well when I would go with the butcher's wife in a van to the outlying villages. She had started driving in London during the war and had never passed a test, so the van was covered in dents and scrapes where she had hit fences and hedges and couldn't reverse to save her life. I would stand on the back of the van holding the back doors wide open so she could turn round and see where she was going, and I would have to shout stop when she got too close to the hedge.

While I was working there I had a rather unfortunate experience. It was one Christmas eve and I had been plucking chickens all day ready for customers after Christmas. At about eight pm the butcher told me I had better be getting home. There were no street lights in the village and the night was very dark with no moon, but I knew that if I kept my eye on the sky, I would just be able to see the outline of a telegraph pole. If I kept to the left of that I would turn into my road and would see the lights of my home. I was running fast and as I got to the telegraph pole I hit a nineteen fifty's car with a straight up back that had been parked there with no lights on. I had literally run into a car. I hit it so hard that the owners who were visiting the nearest house heard the bang from indoors and came out so see what had happened. They found me laying knocked out in the middle of the road. I had badly cut both knees and cut and broken my nose. They took me home and I was patched up and proceeded to have the most miserable Christmas of my life!

The most enjoyable job I had as a child was at the cinema on the Army camp, today it would never be allowed. At the age of thirteen myself and two brothers, John (also thirteen) and Jimmy Green (fourteen) were offered a job at the army cinema as ushers. It was run for the Army Kinema Corporation by a civilian manager and his wife. It showed two films a night with a change of program every night and our job was to tear the tickets and let the soldiers in.

The cinema was virtually full every night. There were two classes of seat, about five rows of plush seats at the back which cost two shillings and tenpence and the rest were rows of fold-up wooden chairs which cost one shilling and eightpence. Obviously, most of the soldiers bought the cheap seats and stayed there until the lights went down. At this point they would get up and cross the wide gap to the expensive seats. What they did not realise was that, our eyes had grown accustomed to the darkness and we could see.

We stood just inside the doors with our rubber flashlights at the ready and as they made their move we would switch on our torches and catch them midway across the gap like rabbits caught in a car's headlights. Their training would come into play and they would freeze. We would shout to them to get back and they would creep sheepishly back to their seats. Sometimes we were met with a few choice words telling us to mind our own business and so we would leave. About ten minutes later the lights would suddenly go up and a military policeman would enter the cinema, truncheon in hand, and demand to see tickets. This led to the miscreants either slouching back to their proper seats or being ejected from the cinema. Then the lights would go down again and we would carry on with the film.

Another job it was agreed we would do was sell ice-creams in the interval. Jimmy, being the oldest one and a big lad for his age, volunteered to do it. So, as the lights went up on our first night Jimmy appeared from a door beside the stage with his tray of ice-creams round his neck. There was an almighty rush and within a few seconds Jimmy stood there with an empty ice-cream tray and not a penny taken. Not to be beaten the next night we tried a different tack. We fixed a trestle table to the wall behind the door and, as the lights went up, we pushed the door open. There was a tremendous rush as they tried to push the table back but we managed to hold them. From then on there was a sign in the foyer stating that unless there was an orderly queue no more ice-creams would be sold. We never had any trouble after that.

Up in the projection room were two enormous projectors that stood from floor to ceiling and were operated by winding two carbon rods together until they ignited. They were very dangerous and we were fascinated by them and spent as much time in there as we could. We didn't have a resident projectionist but there was always a soldier on the camp who could operate them so they would be paid to come in each night to run the films.

One night no-one turned up and the manager was left with a cinema full of paid customers and no projectionist. We offered to do it and, faced with having to give all the soldiers their money back the manager agreed. To our amazement everything went smoothly and we were given the job every time a projectionist didn't appear. Things didn't always go smoothly though.

One thing to keep an eye on was that a whole film was usually on three reels, so a few seconds before the end of a reel a small circle would flash at the top right-hand corner of the screen to tell you to throw the switch to the other projector. If we didn't keep a close eye on the reels we would miss this and suddenly the screen would just turn white and the film would stop. This would lead to uproar in the auditorium until we got the second projector started and the film continued. Another more serious problem with the projectors was overheating. The first thing you would see was the film on the screen turn a slightly brown colour, usually from one corner, then the whole thing bursting into flames. Once again uproar from the soldiers. We had one record which was very popular at the time called "Tom Hark". We would immediately put this on and the soldiers would clap, stamp and whistle to it while we put out the fire, cut and re-splice the film, start up the projectors again and get the film running. The record lasted two minutes and forty seconds and we never failed to get the film running again before it ended. Over the years when I have heard that piece of music either on the radio or, more likely, on the fairground or amusement arcade my memory goes back to those days.

At the end of the night the rule was to always put the reels of film on a spindle and rewind it to the beginning because it would be going on to another army camp the next morning. Sometimes we would receive a film where this had not been done and when we first started to run the films we did not realise this. So, if we did not notice when loading the film, the lights would go down and the film would start from the end of the reel, running backwards and upside down. We would then have to stop it, unload the projector, rewind the film back to the beginning and then reload it again and start the projector. Believe me you only make that mistake once!

I cannot remember how much we were paid but it was only a few shillings each week, but at the end of each show we collected and shared all the spare change from the floor that had fallen out of the soldier's pockets and we also all had a good assortment of berets, badges and belts.

We saw fourteen films a week, even the "horror" and the "naughty" ones. The manager assured my mother at the start that we would not be allowed to see these but he never stopped us and luckily she never found out. These days Health & Safety would go mad.

After two wonderful years working in the cinema it all had to come to an end as I was leaving home and moving into lodgings in King's Lynn to go to college. During my final year at secondary school we had been visited by a careers adviser who had asked me if I knew what work I wanted to do for a living. As my favourite subjects were English language and Art I told him I was interest in going into journalism. He told me I would have to go to college and do a commercial course that included "O" level shorthand and typing. I was thrilled that I would no longer have to do Maths.

I moved into very good lodgings with a retired railway man and his wife in September 1960 and immediately we were given a lecture from the college principal telling us we were no longer school children but were "Students" and should act as adults. He continued by telling us that one of the most important things was to preserve the reputation of the college and wear our full uniform at all times. Let me remind you that at the time we were in the middle of the "Rock 'n Roll" era and the last thing you wanted to be seen in as a teenager was grey flannels and a blue blazer covered in gold braid and a badge.

I would travel home every Friday night after college by bus from King's Lynn to Hunstanton, then changing to another bus to Wells. Unfortunately no buses went further than Wells and my father did not have a car, so every Friday night I had to hitch hike the last four miles to Stiffkey. This was considered perfectly acceptable at the time. Luckily a bus did come through the village on a Sunday evening to take me back again.

I buckled down for the first year and at the end of the year I took my RSA grades one and two and passed all of them with honours and distinction. Then came year two and my hormones were going wild and Rock 'n Roll took me over. Coffee bars and music became my life. My grey flannels were replaced by charcoal grey "drainpipe" trousers and Cuban heeled "winkle pickers" shoes. My white shirt changed to a two-tone green one with tassels across the front and my blazer changed to a lightweight shower-proof jacket with the collar permanently turned up. More than once I was called to the principal's office and given a lecture on my dress and threatened with expulsion but it never happened. At the end of the second year I took six "O" levels and only managed to pass one, English Language.

Before I took my exams I started to enquire about jobs with local, regional and national newspapers, only to be told that to get into journalism you needed to go to university just to get a position as a tea boy in newspaper offices. I had been completely misled by my careers adviser who was obviously totally ignorant of the qualifications needed to get into journalism. So, there I was, in a position where I had taken six "O" levels, had not got the results yet but urgently needed a job. I could not return home as there were no jobs on the north Norfolk coast unless it was on a farm, a factory or a seasonal job by the seaside, and there were already too many applicants for them by people who had not bothered to go to college. So, what should I do?

Chapter 2:

I start my adult working life

My landlord had the answer. "Get a job on the railways, you will have a job for life". I applied and went for my interview in Peterborough, and, on the strength that I had taken six "O" levels I got a job in the parcel's office on King's Lynn railway station. I worked a forty-four-hour, six-day week for four pounds, eleven shilling and eightpence a week. After a few months I was offered promotion. This meant my wages increased to five pounds two shillings and twopence a week but I had to do shift work. I started at six am one week and worked until seven thirty pm the next.

After my first few weeks I was asked if I would like to join the Union. I was not interested in unions so I said "No". I then began to realise that, unless they had to do it for the job, everyone had stopped speaking to me, no social chat, I was ignored, sent to Coventry. After another two or three weeks I was asked by my manager once again if I had reconsidered joining the Union. I said "OK" and everyone started to speak to me again.

I was also introduced to the corruption in the rail industry. Every Friday a carton of scotch pancakes would come through the parcel's office for a café in the town. If the carton was damaged it was not accepted, so every now ang again the carton would be "accidentally" dropped on the floor from a great height and the contents would be shared out between the staff. Sometimes this would happen to a carton of fresh chickens and everyone would have chicken for Sunday lunch. Everybody seemed to be on a "fiddle" some way or another.

One unusual thing I do remember about working at the railway station is that one day a pig arrived by train and the farmer had come to collect it on his own. The pig was a Large White boar and very noisy and everyone was afraid of it, none of the porters would go anywhere near it. I was used to pigs as my father had kept them all through my childhood so I volunteered to help the farmer. He had two large sheets of corrugated iron and we got one each side of the pig and sandwiched it. We then marched off the train with the pig between us, along the platform and straight out of the exit into his truck. No problem!

The best thing to come from my time working for British Railways was I met Suzanne. She was a friend of the girl who worked in the booking office and she used to come and visit in her lunch time. Some people say there is no such thing, but I can tell you it was love at first sight for both of us. We were both seventeen and I was twelve days older than her. We had our first date at a local pub where they had a juke box and we played music all evening and tried to jive. Our next date was to the Corn Exchange in King's Lynn where we saw the amazing Gene

Vincent. It was wonderful to see this great American singer as he had only a few years previously survived the car crash that had killed his great friend Eddie Cochran. Gene had also been badly injured in the crash and only lived another seven years.

We found that our jiving was getting better and by the next dance when we saw Shane Fenton, who years later re-appeared as Alvin Stardust, we won a jiving competition.

Conditions at my lodgings were getting a bit frosty as my landlord still wanted to treat me as if I was at college with a curfew of nine pm and he cross examined me about my girlfriend. I made the mistake of telling him that she had had a lifesaving operation when she was only five years old and had her left lung removed. He immediately forbade me to see her again, which of course I ignored. Life became intolerable so I had to find new lodgings. I was lucky to find more very good lodgings but I had to pay three pounds a week and I was only earning five pounds so money was very tight.

After less than two years I left my job with British Railways and went to work in the factory at Campbell's Soups in King's Lynn in the defrosting section of the vegetable soup production line. This was a completely new experience for me but at the end of the first week I got ten pounds in my pay packet. I paid my landlady and went straight into town and bought a pair of trousers and a jumper.

After five months I was called into the office and was asked what "O" levels I had got because it was on their records that I had a college education and there was a vacancy in the payroll office. I had to admit that I only had one pass and had not even taken Maths as a subject. I don't know what they saw in me but they asked me if I thought I could do the job and I said "Yes, of course", so I was transferred into the office and I did the job very well.

After another five months I was offered a position as Timekeeper back down in the factory, responsible for the warehouse and maintenance staff. This was another promotion with more money so I accepted the position. This meant I was not tied to a desk all day and was able to roam around the factory. I really enjoyed this job and, because I was responsible for the maintenance men I had to go in for two hours every Sunday morning to complete their time cards. The job only ever took me about thirty minutes so, in the summer I used to climb to the top of the famous Campbell's water tower and sunbathe on the top. In the winter I sometimes passed the time away by driving a forklift truck round the warehouse.

By now things with Suzanne were getting very serious and just before Christmas 1963 I asked her to marry me and we got engaged on Christmas day.

Her mother was overjoyed, mine was not so happy as I was still only eighteen but she gave us her blessing anyway. Soon after Christmas a small end of terrace house became available from a member of Suzanne's family. It was in a very bad state of repair but I went cap in hand to my father and asked him if I could borrow four hundred pounds to buy a house. I took my parents to see it and they agreed so, at eighteen I became a property owner. To help with my finances I left my lodgings and moved into my little house with a bed, a settee and a gas ring for cooking.

I also got a Saturday job delivering Corona soft drinks door to door in King's Lynn. I don't remember how much I was paid but it all added to my meagre income. It is strange how some things stay in your mind from many years ago, and I remember a lady once asking me for a bottle of lime juice corduroy. Her teenage daughter, standing beside her said "Mother you're stupid, tha's not corduroy, tha's cordrial!" Our round was through some of the "rougher" parts of Lynn and another thing I remember was going to the back door of a house. The door was slightly ajar with pop music blasting out. I knocked on the door a couple of times before a tiny pair of hands appeared and pulled the door open. It was a scruffy little toddler dressed only in a nappy. I bent down and said to him "Is your mummy in?" and he answered "F*** off".

Suzanne and I were married on the 12th of September 1964 at the age of nineteen and a half with only forty pounds to our name. We had a three-night honeymoon in Great Yarmouth, and so started the most wonderful lifetime together. There was the odd hiccup along the way which I will come to further along in my story.

My income by then had risen to fifteen pounds a week but things were still very tight. We had a back yard with an old lean-to shed along one side. This we proceeded to dismantle and chop into kindling sticks which we bundled and sold to the local shop. Every penny of income was useful as I had recently bought a BSA Bantam motorcycle, and, after about two years I traded it in for a Reliant Regal three-wheeler van.

For our first holiday the year after we were married we went round the coasts of Kent, Sussex and Hampshire to the New Forest, sleeping in the back of our tiny van and cooking outside on a primus stove. Luckily the weather treated us kindly. In the evening we would pull into a suitable field gateway or lane and park up for the night.

Just before our marriage my bosses at Campbell's Soups called me into the office once again and told me they were planning to install a computer, the first one in King's Lynn. Once again what qualifications had I got, did I have "A" level Maths? As usual my answer was "No". For some reason though they asked me if I thought I could do the job and as usual my answer was "Yes". This meant a month after our marriage I was sent off to IBM headquarters in London for three weeks to learn how to program a computer. I will never forget the first night away in a hotel. It was an enormous place with corridors disappearing into the distance. I found my room and went through the door and switched on the light. I was greeted by the sound of rustling as hundreds of cockroaches made a dash for cover. On inspecting the room I found a Gideons bible in a drawer covered in dead crushed cockroaches. It was late on a Sunday evening so I had no choice but to stay there the night. I rang Campbells the next morning and told them I would not be going back there and would be finding another hotel

When I came back to work an enormous computer was installed which required removing part of the roof and lowering it into the office. It was connected to a large tabulator which printed out Invoices, Payroll and Accounts. It was fed by punch cards which were produced by three girls who sat in a row at punch card machines. I was the first person ever to program and run a computer in King's Lynn. Later as two other large companies in the town installed computers I was leased out to program them also. All this coincided with the first pay freeze in the early seventies, and, even though I had gained so many qualifications the company refused to give me a pay rise. Other companies at the time were getting round the pay freeze by "creating" posts that had a higher pay grade, but Campbell's refused this and I was running their computer system on the same pay as when I had been a Timekeeper in the factory.

After two years in our little terraced house, we managed to sell it for six hundred pounds and we moved to a bungalow in Ingoldisthorpe, a village ten miles from King's Lynn and just five miles from the coast. I had in the mean time passed my full driving test and had bought a Ford Thames van and then a Morris Traveller, which we also slept in as we continued on our course round the south and west coast of England and the length of Wales for our holidays.

When I decided to apply for a full driving licence my test came through for nine am on Christmas Eve, which was a Friday. I had been driving my Reliant for about two years on my motorcycle licence but I needed a four-wheel car to take my test in, so I contacted a local driving instructor who had a Ford Anglia. He asked me if I had ever driven one before and I said no so we arranged for me to have a one-hour lesson on the Wednesday evening. At nine am on the Friday I got into the car with the examiner at the test centre and we turned left for South Lynn where I did my emergency stop and reversing round a corner. We then started heading back into the town centre for the main part of the test. We immediately came up behind virtually stationary traffic. By the time we passed the test centre again we were already twenty minutes late for his next test. The examiner said it was hopeless and he would not be able to do any tests today in this traffic and told me to turn into the centre. When I parked the car he handed me a form and said "You'll do, you've passed your test". That was my driving test!

We paid three thousand pounds for the bungalow with a mortgage of two thousand three hundred pounds and seven hundred pounds cash. When the pay freeze came along, I was only earning just over sixteen pounds a week and we struggled to survive. Suzanne had continued to work part time while we were in King's Lynn, but because of her life long health problems she was continually getting chest infections which meant spells in hospital so I was determined that she should not have to work. A colleague of mine at Campbell's had left recently and got a job on the road as a salesman with much better pay, so this got me thinking "I could do that".

I started answering adverts for selling jobs. I went on a two-day training session in Peterborough to learn how to sell an indoor air heating system and soon realised it was never going to work. I applied to a seed merchant who sold seed to farmers in the area and they decided they didn't want me as I had no experience. I eventually got an interview with

Crawford's Biscuits, part of the United Biscuit Company. I was interviewed in a car on the market place in King's Lynn. The manager told me I wasn't selling material and would never be any good at selling. I thanked him for his advice and said I wouldn't be taking it until I had got a job in selling and proved it to myself. This was obviously the right answer because he immediately offered me the job.

I started a month later with a nice new Ford Escort and soon found that I was not bad at selling. I WAS TERRIBLE! I stumbled on from week to week, never reaching my targets. They gave me more training but I still did not improve, and realised during my second year that my days were numbered. I could not bear the thought of going back into an office and my pay would almost certainly drop, so I started to apply for more selling jobs. I had blind faith that in the right job I could be successful.

I eventually got an interview with the local manager for the Prudential Insurance company. He told me I had got the job and would be getting written confirmation by post in the next few days. The next day my manager at Crawford's rang me to tell me that they had decided to end my contract of employment with one month's notice. I was happy to tell him I had in fact got another job so he told me I could leave at the end of the week. I waited for my confirmation to arrive and, after a week I began to get worried that I had not received it, so tried ringing the manager with no success. I eventually managed to speak to his secretary who told me off the record he had changed his mind and given the job to his son-in-law instead. I was desperate, I had a wife to support and a mortgage to pay. Luckily I had kept my old car so at least I had transport.

I did not want to be unemployed for the first time in my life so I visited a friend who worked in the office of a local removals and marquee erection company and asked if he could give me a temporary job while I looked for another one. He took me on and for the next few months I was subjected to the hardest manual work I had ever done in my life. Trying to keep up with hardened removal men was very difficult, the weights they lift are absolutely phenomenal, but having a section of wet canvas marquee loaded onto your back to carry was spine crushing, and all this at a wage so low that meant the longer I worked there the more in debt I was getting.

After five months I managed to find a new position as a salesman for the Independent Order of Foresters, selling door to door insurance on a commission only basis. This was definitely make or break. I was so desperate I took the job. My work consisted of going into the area office in Norwich every Monday morning for an update and to pick up any leads or enquiries, the main part of my income was earned by cold calling. The team consisted of a manager and twelve salesmen who covered the whole of Norfolk. Every week the team changed as people dropped out as their expenses were larger than their sales, but for some reason I found that I could sell and my policies kept rolling in.

The company was run by an eccentric man who stood on stage at the annual conference and asked us if we were insane working for him, and how could we be sure. He then produced release papers from an asylum to prove he was no longer insane and had been cured. He was the only one in the room that had written proof that he was not insane. The characters you meet in selling! I lasted in this job for two years and it was not my fault that it ended. The area manager was paid a percentage of his team's sales and most of the time there were only myself and one other man earning a living wage, so we were earning more that he was. I went into the office one Monday as usual only to be told that the area was not paying for itself so, please leave all documentation there and go home, your employment has ended.

I did not want to go home and tell Suzanne I was out of work again so I drove to King's Lynn and went to the Dornay Foods factory, part of the Mars group that made potato products. I went into the office and asked if there were any jobs going on the production line. The lady asked me if I was a student and I answered "I can be if you like". She laughed and said for my cheek she would take me on a temporary contract canning new potatoes, and when a position came available on the permanent mashed potato line I would be moved onto permanent staff. The only problem was it was shift work which involved three days of six am until two pm, then three days two pm until ten pm, then three nights ten pm until six am, then, in theory, three days off. It doesn't work like that of course because you are asleep for most of your first day off.

I was soon transferred onto permanent staff and was earning a reasonable wage, and, believe it or not, even though I did not like the shift work very much it allowed me to switch my brain off and give it a rest.

I had been working there for nearly two years when I was called into the office and asked questions about my education. I thought "Here we go again". Have I got any "A" levels in maths, chemistry or physics? Once again I said I had not and asked why. They told me they had noticed on my employment records that I had a college education and wondered what my qualifications were because there was a vacancy in the laboratory testing the products, working with other employees who had "A" levels and university degrees. For some reason they wondered if I thought I was capable of doing the job and I of course once again said "Yes". I don't know why they gave me the position, I can only imagine they could not be bothered to advertise outside the company.

The next week I moved into the laboratory where I had to check the contents of tinned potatoes, the weight, saline content in the water and size of the potatoes. I also had to weigh the contents of packets of instant mash and mix with milk to check consistency, (and you needed a university degree to do that?).

A funny thing happened one night while I was working there. Each shift someone from quality control would select a can at random from the retort baskets and test them. A retort basket holds several hundred cans that have been heated to sterilise them. During a shift there would be up to twenty separate retort baskets to choose from.

He randomly chose one tin from the many thousands in front of him and took it into the laboratory. When he opened it he found that inside the tin there was no saline liquid, just one enormous potato that had been carefully cut to fit inside the tin exactly. It had been taken from the separate store where potatoes were kept to produce instant mash and someone had crafted it to fit inside a tin, slipped it onto the production line where it's lid had been fitted and had been sterilised. Of all the thousands of cans produced that night shift this one had been selected randomly for testing. All hell broke loose and the whole night shift production was scrapped. Someone with a warped sense of humour must have been very bored that night.

Chapter 3:

Back on the road again

I had only been working in the laboratory for three weeks when I received a phone call at home from a man who introduced himself and said "You don't know me but I have a man called Ray working for me that used to be your area manager for the "Foresters". I am looking for someone to cover the Norfolk area and he says you are a very good salesman and are desperate to get back into selling. I told him I would discuss it with my wife and get back to him. We had an in-depth discussion and about two minutes later I rang him back and accepted the job.

The next week I started working for the Ansafone Company selling rental contracts for telephone answering machines. In the 1970's it was illegal to purchase and connect an answering machine to a telephone, you could only use a machine from a licenced company who supplied it on a rental basis. The job consisted of following up enquiries plus cold calling on every kind of business and convincing them of the benefits of having an automatic answering machine. The position was salary based with a good commission and I took to it like a duck to water. I was suddenly earning more than I had ever earned before. Every day was different, one day I could be demonstrating my machine to a board of directors and getting signed contracts for several offices, and an hour later I would be pitching the benefits to a jobbing plumber.

One thing customers were very reluctant to do was to record their own answering messages, even though we told them that one of the benefits of the system was that a caller would hear a familiar voice. So, once their machine had been delivered and connected I would go back and record the answering message for them. This meant that after a time my voice was heard all over Norfolk asking callers "not to hang up and please leave a message".

By now our little family was growing and, after several years of trials and tribulations which eventually ended up in Harley Street, in 1974 our son was born, followed a year later by a daughter. Although both sets of parents were overjoyed by these events, my poor father, who had never been out of work in his life, could not understand my way of living and went to his grave still wondering when I was going to get a "proper job".

I used to dismay Peter, my area manager at Ansafone who was ex RAF and spoke with a very "cut glass" accent. If he had one failing it was that when accompanying me on a presentation he could not keep quiet and always tried to "take over". On one visit to a north Norfolk farmer he was strangely quiet and just sat there smiling. After getting a signed contract we left and, in my car, I asked him why he had been so quiet. He told me that immediately I had started to speak to the farmer we had both lapsed into rapid "broad Norfolk" dialect and he couldn't understand a word we were saying, but we were both smiling so he kept smiling also as he guessed things were going well. Thinking about it I suppose that is why I had been so successful selling insurance with the Foresters and then with Ansafone. I was able to easily adapt to my surroundings and build a relationship with the people I was with, whatever walk of life they came from.

I was with Ansafone for four years and by then the market was changing. Cheap illegal answering machines were being imported from the far east and these machines did not rely on tape but were "solid state". Very soon "digital" machines would be coming along and telephones with an answering service built in so it was time to look for pastures new.

I started looking for new job opportunities and eventually noticed an advert in my local paper which said "Hi--- We are an expanding company in the domestic electronics industry and are looking for an ambitious person to open new markets in the Norfolk/Lincolnshire area". This intrigued me so I applied and was asked to go to a hotel in Peterborough for an interview. I was interviewed by my soon to be Regional Manager, Gordon, a man from the northeast of England with very thick lensed glasses. He looked a bit like Hank Marvin from The Shadows. It turned out later that they went to school together and both played in bands while at school. His main claim to fame was that he once auditioned Hank to join their band but turned him down because he was a skinny kid with glasses!

Anyway, back to the interview. We met in a small room in the hotel with Gordon sitting behind a desk and me facing him. I was also sitting in the sun coming through the window and I was wearing Reflectolite glasses which darkened into sunglasses in the sun. So, the first thing I had to do was ask if I could move my chair into the shade so that my glasses could return to normal vision. He was intrigued by them and asked me if they were any good as he had to wear glasses all the time. So, the beginning of the interview was spent demonstrating the virtues of Reflectolite glasses. He told me afterwards that I had already secured the job with my performance selling the virtues of my glasses before getting on to the job itself.

He bought some Reflectolite glasses soon afterwards, but a few months later he was on holiday in Cornwall, swimming in the sea, when a large wave hit him and knocked his glasses off and they were never seen again.

Chapter 4:

An area manager, not just a salesman

The company turned out to be the Japanese company Hitachi, which, by the late seventies had only been in the country for a few years. The range of televisions they were allowed to bring into Britain was restricted to a maximum 19-inch screen size, this was to protect the failing British TV industry. They were also selling a range of radios, cassette recorders, music centres and a small amount of Hifi equipment.

There was a certain amount of negativity in the east of England to Japanese companies as it was still only just over thirty years since the war and the Norfolk and Suffolk regiments suffered particularly badly under the Japanese. He also told me that I would be eventually responsible for over two million pounds of business a year and asked me if I felt I could take the responsibility. My answer was that whether I was selling a product worth one pound or five hundred pounds a sale was still a sale and it was all relative. He offered me the job on the spot and I accepted and it was agreed I would start in April when I would attend their annual conference. I returned home and this time waited for confirmation in writing before handing in my notice with Ansafone.

On my start date I was duly collected by my new regional manager and driven to a large hotel west of

London and got a taste of what it was like working for a large international company. I returned home four days later in a brand-new Ford Cortina.

I already had a reasonable number of accounts spread across my area and I set about opening more. I came across area managers for other companies who were very slick and smart, some of whom were respected but not particularly liked. I decided to continue working in my "friendly" manner and soon gained a large number of loyal retailers. At the beginning I persuaded the local independent dealers that although they did not like Japanese companies the larger chain stores were stocking and selling them and they were losing out. I persuaded them to take in a small stock at first including a couple of televisions and a small selection of other products and see how it went. I knew of course that by the time I called on them a month later at least the televisions would already be sold and they would be asking for more.

My manager who was spending the day with me once told me I was one of the most aggressive salesmen he had ever seen, but it worked because I always did it with a smile on my face and my customers didn't seem to realise what was happening to them!

The Japanese televisions were far more reliable that the British makes and virtually never went wrong. In

1980 we were able to sell as many nineteen-inch screen televisions with only three channels and no remote controls for four hundred pounds each as we were allowed to bring in the country. We had to allocate our share of imports out between our dealers, and at the London trade shows which were held for a week each May in various hotels we would virtually sell out of televisions for the rest of the year.

Our trade shows each year were held in the Cumberland Hotel, Marble arch. One year the hotel asked if they could take some photos of us for promotional purposes and we agreed. I pretended to be demonstrating a video camera to a customer and they took a few photos. I then promptly forgot about it. A year later when I arrived at the hotel I was met by large posters of myself plastered all along the outside walls promoting their commercial and conference facilities. I was never paid any commission!

Another benefit of being in London for a week was that my manager and I could indulge in our love of live music, and every year we spent one night at Ronnie Scott's jazz club. We saw some superb acts over the years including The LA Four, Dizzie Gillespie and several more American and great British artists.

As our business grew we began to purchase spare allocations from other Japanese companies and after ten years we controlled over fifty percent of the British television market. A position, it turned out, very dangerous to be in, but more of that later.

In the early days of working for the company Hitachi had a scheme where they would send about fifteen members of head office and warehouse staff to Japan each year, all expenses paid. The sales staff, however, had to earn their place and a ten-month long competition was set.

It was a known fact that no-one in their first year with the company had ever qualified. After about six months of the competition an area manager who came from Canada was so far in the lead he could not be caught and I was just behind him. He was not a popular member of the sales team and senior management decided to change the rules. It was announced that circumstances beyond their control concerning the availability of product through the selling period etc. etc. had made the rules of the competition unfair and had to be re-drawn. We were then sent a revised list that showed that the Canadian colleague had dropped to about half way down the salesforce and I was immediately below him. He was so enraged by this that he walked out of the company. At the end of the competition the winning two sales managers were announced. I was then told quietly to pack my bags, I was also going to Japan with them. So off we went, a group of nineteen of us from Heathrow airport to Japan.

Even then things didn't go completely smoothly. We left Heathrow on a Jumbo at about midday on the Saturday and flew over the north pole and prepared to land at Anchorage airport in Alaska about twelve hours later for re-fuelling. But as we had flown over the pole we landed only an hour after we had taken off!!!. We approached the airport by turning across the side of some mountains and we hit an air pocket and dropped sideways out of the sky. By the time the pilot had corrected the Jumbo it had lost too much height but he decided to land it anyway.

We hit the runway with an almighty bang and continued along the tarmac towards snow, rocks and the sea. As we approached the end of the runway we were meant to turn right and taxi down to the terminal building. Unfortunately we had hit the runway so hard it had destroyed the steering mechanism and we carried straight on and ploughed into the snow. We sat there for about an hour before being towed backwards to the terminal building where we were offloaded from the plane.

We were given no information so we just sat there until about six pm when we were informed that planes could not take off from the airport after then because the runway froze over every night. We were informed that JAL airlines were trying to find us accommodation in Anchorage overnight. By now we had been awake all night because for us six pm in

Anchorage was five am in London, also all our luggage was still on the plane.

At seven pm we were informed that rooms for all 246 passengers had been found at the Anchorage Hilton Hotel, obviously it must have been a slow night for them! The company was now trying to arrange for a fleet of yellow school buses to transport us to central Anchorage. We were also informed that as none of us were an American citizen we would all have to complete an application form for a twenty-four-hour Visa to enter the United States and also surrender our passports.

Our buses finally arrived at nine pm and off we went into Anchorage. As we were leaving the airport we had to walk down a corridor to the exit and we passed a girl in a cigarette kiosk. As each of us individually passed her she announced "Have a nice day"! Even though it was past nine on Saturday night and, to us, was about eight am Sunday morning. How nobody thumped her I will never know.

The Hilton hotel laid on a buffet meal for us, plus basic washing things and toothbrushes and toothpaste and we crawled off to bed. The time lapse meant after about two hours I was wide awake again so I decided to get dressed and go out and explore Anchorage. As I walked down the street I kept recognising people from the plane, so obviously we were all having the same problem sleeping.

The next morning after a good breakfast we were loaded back onto the school buses, still wearing the same clothes we had worn yesterday, and taken back to the airport. The first flight in from Japan in the morning had brought the necessary spare parts to repair our Jumbo and we took off at twelve midday on Sunday. We then flew over the international date line and landed at Tokyo airport at five pm on Monday. (Confused or what).

Once through customs we were loaded into a coach and taken to the New Otani hotel in the centre of Tokyo. Our guide told us that because we were very late we were just to drop our luggage into our rooms and get back on the coach again for a city tour. He was told in no uncertain terms what he could do with his city tour! Such a shame as, being Japanese, he was being very polite.

Our first week in Japan was hectic as we travelled all over the country visiting their various factories, including Hitachi city with a population of 170,000 and the home of the most gigantic "white goods" factory. It took us all day to just walk round the washing machine production line.

We had the privilege of seeing new products and innovations at various factories that would be several years before they reached the market in Britain, including liquid crystal screened televisions that could be hung on the wall, flat speakers and even something called "video recorders". It was fascinating considering this was over forty years ago.

At the weekend we boarded the famous "Bullet Train", also built and operated by Hitachi, and headed from Tokyo to the ancient capital of Kyoto in the south. Although it was now March they were suffering from an unusually late heavy snowfall and the Bullet Train, renowned for always being on time, was running late. Everything was controlled from a central base in Tokyo and it was announced in Japanese of course that to save time the doors would only be opened at Kyoto station for thirty seconds instead of the usual one minute.

We duly arrived at the station and only about half our party, complete with luggage had managed to leave the train when the doors closed and it started to pull out of the station. One of our party still on the train, we never discovered who it was, panicked and pulled the communication cord. All hell broke loose as the Japanese staff panicked as I should not think it had ever happened before. Control back in Tokyo was contacted and it was decided that the train should reverse back into the station and the doors would be opened again. Before this could happen another train running behind had caught up with us and was also trying to enter the station, so this train also had to be reversed to let our train back in. Eventually it was all sorted out and our party was reunited and we sheepishly left the station and boarded a coach to our hotel.

We had a fascinating weekend visiting ancient Shinto and Buddhist temples, and also the famous Mirror Temple, but we did not see it mirrored in the lake as the water was completely frozen over. We also visited a typical Japanese teahouse and had green tea seated on cushions around a low table, served by a "geisha" in traditional costume. Then on the Monday we went back to visiting Hitachi factories in the south of the country before eventually heading back to Tokyo.

Because of the heavy snow Mount Fiji was particularly spectacular as we passed it on the train.

One train we travelled on was called "The Kinki Nippon Railway" which amused our British sense of humour but obviously meant something completely different in Japanese.

After two weeks our fascinating and hectic tour of Japan was over and we boarded a plane to Hong Kong where we stayed for a couple of day's rest. While there we managed to fit in a tour of the harbour area and an evening meal in a floating restaurant. Then on to Singapore where Hitachi also had a factory. As well as visiting this factory we had a lovely few days being guided round Singapore and it's superb Orchid Gardens and Chinese Quarter, plus a rickshaw convoy to the famous Raffles Hotel.

Here we sat on the terrace in the gardens drinking "Gin Slings" and enjoying High Tea.

Eventually it was time to head home and we arrived at Heathrow three weeks after we had left, very tired but with memories we would never forget.

Two years later I was top salesman and won a European holiday of my choice. Suzanne and I went for a week in August to the Bernese Oberland in Switzerland. We booked our suitcases into Heathrow and took a flight to Berne. We then transferred to a train to Interlaken where we transferred to another train to take us up to Grindelwald. We were then met by a minibus and driven to our hotel and, as if by magic, our suitcases appeared from the back of the minibus. How efficient are the Swiss? Our hotel in Grindelwald overlooked the north face of the Eiger mountain.

Every day included a train ride to the top of a different mountain. One train took us through the Eiger itself and up to the "Top of Europe" on the permanent glassier with its famous observatory standing on a ridge near the top and a large ice tunnel and cave which housed many wonderful ice sculptures. At the top of one mountain we visited there was a festival and we even came across a youth brass band from England performing in the sunshine. Another highlight of our holiday was a heart-stopping cable car ride from one mountain to the top of another to visit the revolving restaurant that had recently featured in a James Bond film. The weather was kind to us with unbroken sunshine every day.

Over the next few years I was never out of the top five in the salesforce and during this time I also won two supermarket dashes and a trip to Denmark. Unfortunately the Denmark trip did not turn out as smooth as planned. I had to drive from Norfolk all the way to our head office in Hayes, Middlesex where I boarded a coach which took our small group all the way back to Harwich. A colleague of mine was absolutely terrified of flying and was so relieved that we were going by ferry.

When we arrived at Harwich we were informed that the "Dana Anglia" ferry had engine problems and was running several hours late. It finally arrived at five pm and we left at six pm, five hours late. We were informed that one of the engines had stopped working so we were going on half power and this meant the stabilizers were not working either. The crossing was horrific. I can't remember how long it took us now but it seemed to last forever. Everyone was ill and we were eventually very glad to get off the boat at Esbjerg and onto a coach to take us up to Ringkobing which was the home of a sister companies' factory which made Hifi and speaker cabinets.

By now we had lost almost a day so our hosts decided to change the itinerary. We were now going to stay in Denmark an extra day, including a visit to Copenhagen, then go home by plane! To my friend's horror we were also travelling from Ringkobing to Copenhagen by plane, and when we arrived at the airport we were met by a small blue "Shorts of Belfast" prop plane. We boarded the plane and as we were taxiing along the runway the pilot joked to us that as he took off he would shout and we all had to jump at the same time to get off the ground. To say my friend was terrified would be an understatement.

We had a lovely day in Copenhagen and I had a photo taken with "The Little Mermaid" and we visited the Royal residence. In the evening we were hosted by the company's managing director to a meal and entertainment.

The next morning as we headed for the airport to fly home the wind was blowing a gale. We boarded the plane and flew back to Heathrow. As we made our approach our plane was pitching and bucking and it was obvious the pilot was having trouble keeping it under control. I was sitting at a window seat on the right of the plane and my friend was crouching down beside me. I looked out of the window and saw a runway going off to the right of us at an angle of about forty-five degrees. I then suddenly realised that this was the one we were trying to land on. We eventually set down and the plane lurched from side to side as we waltzed along the tarmac.

Eventually we stopped, and as we were leaving the plane the pilot stood at the door looking ashen faced and apologised to everyone for the landing and two of the stewardesses were even in tears. We were told afterwards that we had been the last plane to be allowed to land before they closed the airport. I don't know if my friend ever flew again!

About this time Hitachi became the first company to sponsor a football team. Liverpool was our choice as they were winning everything and, at the same time conquering Europe. As part of the deal we were allocated tickets to matches, and I would fill my car with dealers and drive the two hundred miles to Liverpool. We would park at a hotel on the outskirts of the city and have a drink before being taxied to Anfield. Here we would be treated to a four-course meal with wine in the trophy room before going out to watch the first half. Half time it was back into the trophy room for more drinks then out for the second half. At the end of the game back inside we went again for another drink before being taxied back to our hotel. Here we would be joined by at least two of the players for a few more drinks before getting in my car and driving home to Norfolk again! How did we get away with it?

On one visit to Anfield a dealer had brought his eight-year-old son to the game. He was already a staunch Liverpool fan and was dressed in full kit. The promotions manager had promised to get him some players' autographs but it was getting close to kick-off had he was nowhere to be seen. I asked the boy if he would come with me and we went to the player's dressing room. The door was guarded by a large security guard and I told him my problem. To my amazement he said that I had better hurry as they would be going out for the game soon and opened the door for us. We were surrounded by "The Dream Team". I approached Ray Clements, who I had previously met, and he took us round the room to get all the autographs, including the little boy's hero, Kenny Dalgleish. As we went back to the stands I don't think that little boy's feet touched the ground.

We always had a larger allocation of tickets when Liverpool played Norwich City and I would be able to take about a dozen guests. The only problem was they were all City supporters and we had to sit with the Liverpool fans. I always had to wear my company blazer of course and was picked out by the fans for a bit of banter. At one game they kept asking me to sell them my blazer. This I could not do but, as a laugh, I decided to auction off my company tie. I cannot remember how much I got for it, but about three months later, at our annual conference, the sales director announced that we would be having a new outfit ready for the trade shows in May including a new company tie. He then said "I know Ken needs a new one because he sold his last one at a football match". How do they find out these things?

I got my own back on him later when he and the financial director were supposed to be spending a few days at the Scotland distribution centre. I was setting up for an evening Hifi demonstration at the Barnham Broom Golf & Leisure Club in Norfolk when they both came walking through the door in full golfing gear and clubs on their backs. All my expenses went on his account that night!

Suzanne and I also had a wonderful holiday in Kenya during that time with a week's safari in the Maasai Mara followed by a week at Mombasa Beach. We were building more memories.

Back at work things started to go wrong. As I mentioned earlier, we had grown to be the biggest sellers of televisions in the country with a fifty-two percent share of the market. The British television industry was dying on its feet and two of our main Japanese competitors had got round the import restrictions by building factories in Britain. If we had built a factory as well it could have ended in political unrest, so we took the only other option to us and took over the failing factory of a British company in south Wales which was about to close down. It turned out to be the worst thing we could have done.

Chapter 5:

A rather disturbing incident

I think this is a good time to mention an incident in our lives that happened in 1980. I was in London at my annual trade show and Suzanne was at home with the children. When I went away for any length of time her mother came to stay with her to help.

One morning the front doorbell rang and when she opened the door she was confronted by a policeman who asked "Is your husband at home?"

She answered "No, he is at work"

"When will he be home?"

"Not till Friday, he is away in London at a trade show"

"Does he go away often?"

"Now and again. What is this all about?! She asked.

He answered "I can't tell you, please just answer my questions".

By now Suzanne was getting quite worried.

Can you describe him, how tall is he?"

"Five feet eight" she answered.

"Dark or fair hair?"

"Dark" she answered.

"Straight or curly?" he asked.

"Curly" mother-in-law said, "he's got a perm."

"No, it's straight at the moment" Suzanne corrected. He has had a perm for the past two years but he has recently had it cut out.

"Why?" asked the policeman.

"He got fed up with it" she answered.

"Clean shaven or beard?" he asked.

"He's had a beard for the last two years but he shaved that off as well two weeks ago" she answered.

"Why?" Asked the policeman.

"Because I didn't like it" she answered.

"So, you are telling me that in the past couple of weeks he has completely changed his appearance".

"Yes, I suppose so" she answered, "Please what is this all about?"

"I can't tell you, just answer my questions" he said.

"Next question, does he own a green estate car?"

"Yes" my mother-in-law said "It's parked on the drive".

"No it's not, Mum" Suzanne said, "He sold it a couple of weeks ago."

At which point the policeman started to get a bit agitated and asked her if she knew who I had sold it to?

"Yes, his sister" she said.

"Please ring her immediately, I need to speak to her" he said

Suzanne rang her and the policeman took over, and after confirming her name and address told her not to touch the car until the police had inspected it.

By now Suzanne and her mother were getting frantic.

"One more question" he said. "Does your husband ever go and stay away up north, and was he there last August/September?"

"Yes" Suzanne said, "He was at the Harrogate Hifi Show sometime last September but I don't remember the dates."

The policeman told them he promised he would be back the next day to tell them what it was all about, and left.

Suzanne and her mother were beside themselves with worry. I rang them every night but they dare not tell me what had happened because they knew I would rush straight home. So they had a very sleepless night.

True to his word the policeman returned the next morning and told them I had been eliminated from their enquiries as the Harrogate dates did not match up with their investigations.

Suzanne asked him again what was it all about?

He told her that they were checking up on the owners of every green estate car in the country in the hunt for the so-called "Yorkshire Ripper!"

After seeing pictures of Peter Sutcliffe when he was finally arrested it was amazing how similar we had looked. I was the same height and same colour hair. I had had a beard and curly hair but had suddenly completely changed my appearance, had recently sold the very model car they were investigating, and I had been in the Yorkshire area.

If the car had been in my drive they would have opened the back door and the first thing they would have seen would have been a hammer. I used to use the car to go to the beach and always carried a hammer to knock the windbreak into the sand.

It all ended well for me at the time, but it just shows how easily people can be wrongfully arrested.

Chapter 6:

Back to my story, things rapidly go downhill

As hard as the Japanese managers tried, they could not change the work ethic of the British workers. I had seen for myself when visiting a tv factory in Japan that to enter the production area you had to wear white coveralls, overshoes and head covering. In south Wales the women on the production line wore ordinary clothes, were allowed to smoke and, every Friday the local butcher was allowed to go along the production line selling meat for the weekend. I promise you this is true.

Suddenly the quality and reliability of Hitachi television went through the floor. Quality control was hopeless and many televisions came off the end of the production line faulty. These were put aside to be run through the line again. It was finally discovered that at the end of a shift, if production numbers had not been met, some of the faulty ones would be added to the line. This meant that production was knowingly sending out faulty televisions to our customers. My largest customer who I had built up an annual turnover with of over one million pounds once received a batch of twelve televisions and every one was faulty. It was totally unacceptable and a complete nightmare. Within a few months Hitachi's reputation as a quality manufacturer was completely lost. So after twelve wonderful years with this incredible company I decided it was time to look for another job and move on.

At our next monthly meeting I confided to my colleague (the one who hated flying) that I was looking for another company and he shocked me by telling me he had the opposite problem. He had already gone for interviews with two separate companies and had been offered a job with both of them. He could not decide which to take, so, as he lived in Loughton in Essex at the bottom of my area, I asked him whichever he decided to go for, would he recommend me for the other one. A few days later I had a phone call from the national sales manager of AEG (UK) Ltd asking me to go for an interview at their head office in Slough.

AEG was a top German company selling quality white goods to electrical retailers and kitchen studios. I went for the strangest interview I had ever had because it was obvious from the moment I walked in that unless I had two heads or something they had already decided to offer me the job. I walked out of the office with acceptance letters in hand and a start date in four weeks' time.

I soon realised that working for a German company was completely different to working for the Japanese. Whereas the atmosphere at Hitachi had always been friendly and constructive, at AEG it was just the opposite and the whole company had a very negative attitude about it. Fortunately I was able to rise above this and my sales results were good. I called on many of my old Hitachi dealers and persuaded them to open up accounts with AEG as well. I was even able to achieve my monthly sales targets by usually working only four days a week (although my managers never realised this). Still, it was not pleasant working for a company with a mainly negative attitude.

For all the stories of super German efficiency I would like to tell you my experience. The whole salesforce was in Cologne at a trade show in the convention centre and we were sleeping on a boat on the Rhine. The first morning a coach arrived to take us to work, All the driver had to do was drive a few metres down the road, over a bridge and up the other side to where we were working. We boarded the coach and drove over the bridge, turned right and promptly ran out of diesel! The driver had to go and get a can of diesel but still he could not get the coach started again, so eventually he had to call for a replacement coach. We were very late for the start of the trade show.

Another time we spent a whole Trade Show at the NEC in Birmingham with no stock. The company was mid-way between changing its range and none of the new range was ready yet and they decided it was no use displaying the old range. We were part of the

Daimler-Benz group that included Mercedes, so we spent the whole week with a "Silver Arrow" racing car sitting in the middle of an empty stand.

Chapter 7:

A complete change of direction.

Suzanne and I were both keen leisure cyclists and, during my last year with Hitachi, we had set up a company called Norfolk Cycling Holidays as a hobby. We would provide cycles with panniers for luggage, a route map with information on places of interest to visit enroute and we booked bed and breakfast accommodation for each night in advance. Customers would arrive on a Saturday afternoon and we would fit them up with their cycles and holiday information and they would leave their car with us and off they would go. I designed and illustrated a brochure which I lodged and advertised with the East Anglian Tourist Board and also advertised with cycling magazines. We started to get a steady trickle of customers through the first summer and everyone thoroughly enjoyed their holidays, and some even returned to cycle different routes each year. The most frequent phrase we heard from our customers at the end of their holidays was "I always thought Norfolk was flat"

As the company developed we discovered that there was a need for luggage transfer from one lodgings to the next to save people having to carry their own luggage, so this we incorporated into our holidays at an extra charge. Once we had set up luggage transfer we were also able to sell walking holidays as well. We were blessed with two wonderful long-distance walks in the area, Peddar's Way Roman Road from Thetford in the south to the north Norfolk coast and the beautiful Norfolk Coast Path from Hunstanton to Cromer.

I also published a booklet about this time called "Twelve Cycle Rides from King's Lynn and Hunstanton" and placed it in the local tourist information offices, campsites etc. I eventually sold over one thousand copies.

Although we were kept very busy all summer, after the first three years it was obvious it was never going to develop into a stand-alone business but it was taking up all our spare time. By then I was also very unhappy with my job with AEG Ltd and once again fate stepped in.

Out of the blue we received a letter from the Forestry Commission telling us that they were opening a new visitor centre in Thetford Forest in south Norfolk, the largest lowland forest in Britain, and were looking for a company to run a mountain bike franchise. Suzanne and I sat down and had a long discussion about our finances and life values and decided that, as the mortgage had finished and our two children had both left home, we could live on a lot less money and could enjoy a better quality of life together. I wasn't rash. I accepted the franchise and, for the first year, I did the mountain bike hire at weekends and continued to work for AEG, although I must admit they were getting less and less of my time.

We started at High Lodge on the Good Friday with six mountain bikes I had hired from a cycle shop in Cambridge and it poured with rain all day and we didn't hire out a single bike. On the Saturday, Sunday and Monday, however, it was fine and sunny and our bikes were out continually all day. It was obviously going to be a success so the next day I ordered twelve mountain bikes from the shop in Cambridge and also bought the six from them that I had hired. We thought we would be busy during the summer when the visitor centre was open and do our own thing in the winter. How wrong could I be. At the end of the season, even though the visitor centre was closed, people still came to hire bikes and we were busy every weekend through the winter.

A month before the next Easter I went to AEG head office in Slough for our usual over organised and time wasting two-day monthly meeting and handed in my notice. The National Sales Manager was shocked and asked me where I was going. I told him what I was doing and he laughed in my face and asked why I was giving up a good secure job for a flight of fancy, was I suffering from midlife crisis? The news spread through the office like wildfire and the rest of the salesforce were split between some thinking I had gone mad and the rest congratulating me and wishing me success. As fate would have it, a few months after I left them AEG's parent company Deutsch Aerospace urgently needed extra finance and decided to sell AEG to Electrolux to raise cash, and, from what I heard, most, if not all the AEG salesforce were made redundant.

Ever since the first two cars I had owned, all the rest had been estate cars, even my company cars, for the very reason that we continued to explore the coasts and national parks of Great Britain and Ireland and usually slept in our car. Later they came in even more useful for transporting bikes and luggage.

In the early 1970's we started to follow the trend and went on package holidays to all three Balearic Islands and the Spanish mainland. After the children were born and out of nappies we went on to other parts of Spain, France, Gibraltar, Morocco, Tunisia and the Greek Islands. Also, at the same time taking the children all over the UK. They loved the wild places just as much as we did.

Once we started our mountain bike business we thought we would be quiet in the winter months so we took on a couple of rounds delivering the local free newspaper door to door. It was also a very good form of exercise. We never touched the money we earned from this but let it accrue in a bank account. Amazingly, after a time we had enough to pay for a two-week holiday in Thailand. We spent three days in Bangkok, toured round the northern mountainous parts of the country right up to the Golden Triangle and the Burmese border, then five days down south on the wonderful Krabi Beach. We fell in love with Thailand. We even had our picture in the free paper we delivered riding an elephant.

We were now so busy at High Lodge that we were forced to put the holiday business on the back burner and expanded our cycle hire business to include guided tours round the forest for school groups etc. I got leaflets into every school in Norfolk and north Suffolk and the bookings came rolling in. If a party of twenty to thirty came in we would split them in two groups and one would go off orienteering while I took the other group round the forest paths with a bit of exciting single-track racing at the end, then we would stop for lunch and change over and do it all over again. Sometimes if a very large group came in, I would do three circuits in one day plus fitting them all with the correct size bikes and helmets. I soon became very fit and lost a lot of the weight I had put on driving sixty thousand miles a year for AEG.

I employed the son of the café manager, also a keen mountain biker, to help me one or two days a week and I covered the rest of the week with Suzanne helping me every Sunday which was always busy, rain or shine. The school groups even extended into the winter and weekends were always busy. One of the things we enjoyed best was on a Sunday evening when all visitors had gone. We would put all the bikes away, just leaving two out, and we would go for a quiet ride round the forest. We would see the odd weasel or stoat, hares, fallow and red deer with their magnificent antlers, even foxes with their cubs playing on the grassy tracks and enjoying the evening sunshine. Also plenty of rabbits and continuous birdsong, it was heaven.

It was too good to last, however, and at the end of the third year I had a hard battle with the Forestry Commission who wanted to increase my charges considerably. I eventually came to an agreement with them for another year with a further review at the end of that year.

All my bikes were stored in a specially strengthened sea container which I had paid for and had installed myself. On the second of January I had a phone call from the Forestry office telling me to get there quickly, I had had a break-in. When I arrived I discovered that a team had been there with a lorry and an angle grinder and had cut through the entrance gates and the solid steel of my container to get to the bikes. They had stolen about fifty bikes, some brand new, all my tools and repair equipment, they had even stolen the hosepipe I used to clean the bikes with. I could not get insurance because of the remoteness of the site. The police would not even bother to investigate if the alarm went off in the visitor centre. They did inspect my storage container and told me that I had done everything I could to secure it, and apart from building a brick structure nothing else could be done. I was out of business.

The Forestry Commission got another company to replace me and they brought their bikes in every day on a lorry, but after about two years they relented and built a brick bike shop and store onto the side of the centre building which was timber framed. Even then, less than a year after it was built, someone stole a car and drove it straight through the wall and into the shop.

Chapter 8:

Another complete change

I had a friend in my village where I live who had retired from the local college and had bought an eleven-seat minibus and used it for the odd day trip out, about one trip a week, for local retired people. Just before Christmas I had heard that he had an inoperable brain tumour. I took a big deep breath and knocked on his door. I sat and had a chat with him and his wife about his situation and then I told them what had just happened to me and asked them what they intended to do with their minibus. He told me he had offered it to a local business that hired out minibuses for self-drive but they were holding out for the price to go down. I asked them if I offered them the asking price and promised to continue his business would he sell it to me. They agreed and I went to my bank that day and secured a covering loan and the next day I was the owner of a minibus.

I knew that I would have to get a commercial driving licence but I managed to insure it through Norfolk Cycling Holidays which still existed as a company. I was totally ignorant about the fact that I also needed an Operator's Licence and maintenance contract with a local garage and a certificate of worthiness for the minibus. The thing that would make it work was if I could also secure the contract with Norfolk Lavender of Heacham to do the minibus tours to their enormous fifty-acre field on the Royal Sandringham Estate for the seven weeks each summer when the lavender was in flower. My predecessor had done this and so I arranged a meeting with the managing director and secured the contract. Out & About Luxury Minibus Travel was now in business.

I contacted all my predecessor's customers and told them I had taken over the business and also placed an advert in the local free paper which was delivered to every door in the area. The response was instant and I started to do about three trips a week, varying from Norwich shopping trips to mystery tours and Sunday lunch trips. Luckily I had been on the road for so long I knew every town in the area and all the quiet country roads and places to visit.

Things went very well until I was doing my lavender tours in the summer and a DVLA (driver and vehicle licencing agency) officer came to me and asked to see my licence. I was completely stumped and did not know what he was talking about. He then told me that I was driving illegally and I told him my story. He obviously must have taken pity on me because he said he would have to report me to the courts for driving without proper insurance and the correct documentation, but would visit me the next day at home to help me through all the requirements needed. This he did and we went through everything I needed to know to continue my business. He also suggested a driver training company in

Cambridgeshire where I could have a crash course to obtain a restricted PSV driving licence. I asked him what I could do about my Norfolk Lavender contract and he assured me that as he had already spoken to me, he would not be around to see me for at least three months. He also hinted that the reason he had called on me in the first place was that he had been tipped off by another local minibus hire company. I will always be grateful to him for not closing me down on the spot and putting me out of business.

I immediately contacted the driver training company and a month later I had passed my PSV driving test. I had also filled in the reems of paperwork required to obtain an operator's licence, so by the time my court appearance arrived I was running a legal business.

I went before the magistrates in King's Lynn supported by Suzanne, and my solicitor stated the facts about what had happened to me over the past year. Although he agreed that ignorance was not a defence in law, he felt I had been given wrong information when I purchased the minibus and he begged them for lenience. Also, since being stopped I had done everything required to run a lawful business. Luckily the magistrates agreed and gave me a discharge for everything except my wrong insurance which by law had a minimum statutory fine. I agreed to pay the fine immediately and left the court feeling a very lucky person. From that moment on my business went from strength to strength, and within a year I had traded in the eleven-seat minibus for a brand new fifteen-seat Ford Transit.

Once again fate stepped in, and after about three years I noticed that when I walked our dog each morning I was getting a pain between my shoulder blades. If I stopped for a few seconds it went away again, only to return after a minute or two. I decided to see my doctor and he sent me to King's Lynn hospital who arranged for me to visit the Papworth Hospital in Cambridgeshire for an angiogram. My appointment came through on the Monday before Christmas and it was discovered to my horror that I needed a double heart bypass, and in those days the wait for an operation was a year. I was finally paying for all the years of tearing round East Anglia in a company car with little exercise and living on unhealthy food. I could even have dropped dead on my mountain bike!

That was the end of my business. I announced in the press that because of ill health I could no longer continue and was immediately contacted by another local bus company who offered to take me over. I would continue to run my trips for a small wage and they would provide a driver and take the profits. After my operation I could then start driving again. This was a lifeline to me and seemed like a good solution so I accepted and my trips continued with me accompanying them on some of the days. Thirteen months later at the beginning of January 2000 I was admitted into Papworth on a Monday, had the operation on Tuesday and came home on the Saturday morning. Just six weeks later I got my PSV driver's licence back and was driving the minibus again. In the meantime the company which had taken me over needed a fifteen-seat minibus for a school contract so took mine over and bought me a brand new seventeen seat model.

I had been driving this for about a year when they called me into their office and told me they were going into liquidation the next day. If I would like to take over the purchase agreement for my minibus it would be removed from their accounts and I could continue on my own again. I don't know if this was legal but it worked and I was my own boss again, but with the problem of getting another new Operator's Licence. It took some convincing the authorities that I was no longer connected to the other company and had taken no part in its finances, it seems that they had been sailing pretty close to the wind for a long time concerning running a business. I was eventually given a new Operator's Licence back in my own name.

The secret of our success was that nearly all our customers were people who had retired to West Norfolk from the London or Midlands region and wished to explore the area without having to drive themselves. We were also small enough to pick them up at their door and drop them back home at the end of the day. This meant we built up a strong base of regular customers and it was like a friendly club for them. I also installed a microphone system in my minibuses so we could have some good two-way banter. The laughs we had. I always said I was going to publish a book titled "Things Overheard in a Minibus". Some conversations were crazy.

We also extended our trips to London theatre trips and holidays as far afield as Devon and Cornwall, Wales, the New Forest, the Lake District, Derbyshire and Yorkshire, Lancashire, Northumberland and the Scottish Highlands. These holidays were always fully booked and, of course, always included both myself and Suzanne. She was loved by all our customers and was affectionately known as the minibus courier with no sense of direction! The biggest problem I had was convincing my customers that although they treated it as a club, we were running it to make a living. I must admit though the Out & About years were some of the happiest years of our working life.

Also during these years we managed to fit in another holiday to Thailand and a Fly-drive holiday through the USA's great national parks and down the wild Pacific Way from San Francisco to Los Angeles and Hollywood. Once more building memories. I also managed to fit in a right knee replacement somewhere along the way, but this only stopped me driving for a month.

After we had been running Out & About for twelve years and we were approaching our sixty-third birthdays another problem raised its ugly head. The Government in line with the EU decided to tighten up the rules for bus and coach drivers and this included minibuses as well. The rules were to protect drivers from being overworked and driving too many hours. It also included people that drove and did other work as well i.e., people who worked in a garage or office as well as doing driving. This is where it affected me.

They ruled that if I wished to continue running my business, I would have to go on a training course which would cost me two hundred and fifty pounds to get a Certificate of Competence. Even though I had been running a successful business for twelve years I still needed to acquire a certificate to allow me to continue. I also had to cut my driving hours to include the time I spent in my office planning trips, answering the phone and taking bookings, and I had to guarantee I was getting at least two consecutive days completely off in any two weeks.

To monitor this I would need a digital tachograph installed in my minibus at a cost of about twelve hundred pounds to monitor my driving hours and the number of trips I could do each week would have to be reduced, making the company less profitable. It does not take a genius to work out that running a company with just one minibus with all its running costs will not make a large income. We both agreed that it was not worth it for just two years work as I had definitely decided to retire at sixty-five anyway. So we decided to call it a day, said goodbye to our wonderful band of loyal customers, and did our last trip on Christmas Eve 2008. Many customers had become good friends and remained so until the end of their days.

Chapter 9:

Retirement beckons

A year before we retired we had bought a second-hand campervan, and after a few short breaks in it we went for a holiday in the Lake District. As soon as we arrived the water pump packed up so we had a holiday with no running water. On our way home we stopped at a dealer in Lincoln who looked at our hot water system for us. While they were doing this we investigated their stock of motorhomes and by the end of the day we had traded in our campervan for more than we had paid for it and were now the owners of a motorhome.

After retirement we toured all over Britain including the Highland and islands of Scotland including Skye and Mull, right out to the Outer Hebrides. We wild camped all over Scotland just as we had done many years before in our estate cars. Whenever we went north we always stopped for a few days in our favourite Yorkshire Dales on the way home, we loved Swaledale.

We toured France and Spain. We camped in the Pyrenees in January in the snow and sat in our shirtsleeves in February in the sun on the south coast of Spain. We even drove our campervan back to Switzerland for another lovely summer holiday.

After about eight years of retirement we went on our final long-haul holiday to India. To stand in front of and marvel at the Taj Mahal was the perfect ending to our treks across the world.

The next year Suzanne's health began to fail and her lifelong fight against her lung condition began to take its toll, but we still managed to travel around Britain in the motorhome. She then began to need to have oxygen twenty-four hours a day and special breathing equipment at night. But the Papworth Hospital worked wonders and kept her well and extended her life by at least three years after our local hospital had told us there was no hope.

She remained active to the end and we still toured in our motorhome with an oxygen condenser plugged into the cigarette lighter socket to provide oxygen as we travelled, and campsites with mains electric hook-ups at night. To walk about she had an oxygen cylinder on wheels which she called her dog when she took it for a walk. All her life she had been the most positive person I have ever met and was an inspiration to many people. In the last year of her life we even managed to do the wonderful North Coast 500 around the north coast of Scotland. She was one in a million.

She passed away on the 26th March 2019, just eight days after her seventy-fourth birthday and after fifty-six wonderful years together.

I was now on my own and no longer needed to pick rice. People have told me that I have led an unusual and interesting life and, together with Suzanne, I have packed a lot into it and built many memories. I didn't realise it at the time, I was just trying to make a living for my family and always had an attitude that, when asked, my answer was always "Yes I can".

Looking back at my varied life and the eighteen different employment experiences I have had as a child and an adult, good and bad, I am once again reminded of the words of that taxi drive in Thailand. That no matter what happens to knock you back or change your course through life.....

"There is always rice to pick"